LAINEY

The Pink Flamingo

Karen Riggle

ISBN 979-8-89130-465-9 (paperback)
ISBN 979-8-89130-466-6 (digital)

Christian Faith Publishing
832 Park Avenue
Meadville, PA 16335
www.christianfaithpublishing.com

Printed in the United States of America

For my granddaughter, Lainey, who always does things that best fit her. Just like the flamingo. Love, Gram.

L B R
BIRD
SANCTUARY

Now this is a story about a baby flamingo. If you don't know, when a baby flamingo is born, it is just a gray and white, fuzzy-looking bird. It looks nothing like it does when you see them full-grown.

In a small town in the east, there was the LBR Bird Sanctuary. They take care of unwanted and injured birds. On one such summer day, someone dropped off a baby flamingo. One of the workers, named Katie, saw the little one at their gate entrance. She picked up the little flamingo and said, "Oh, little one, we will take good care of you. Don't be scared." The little flamingo snuggled into Katie's arms. "You seem to feel safe now."

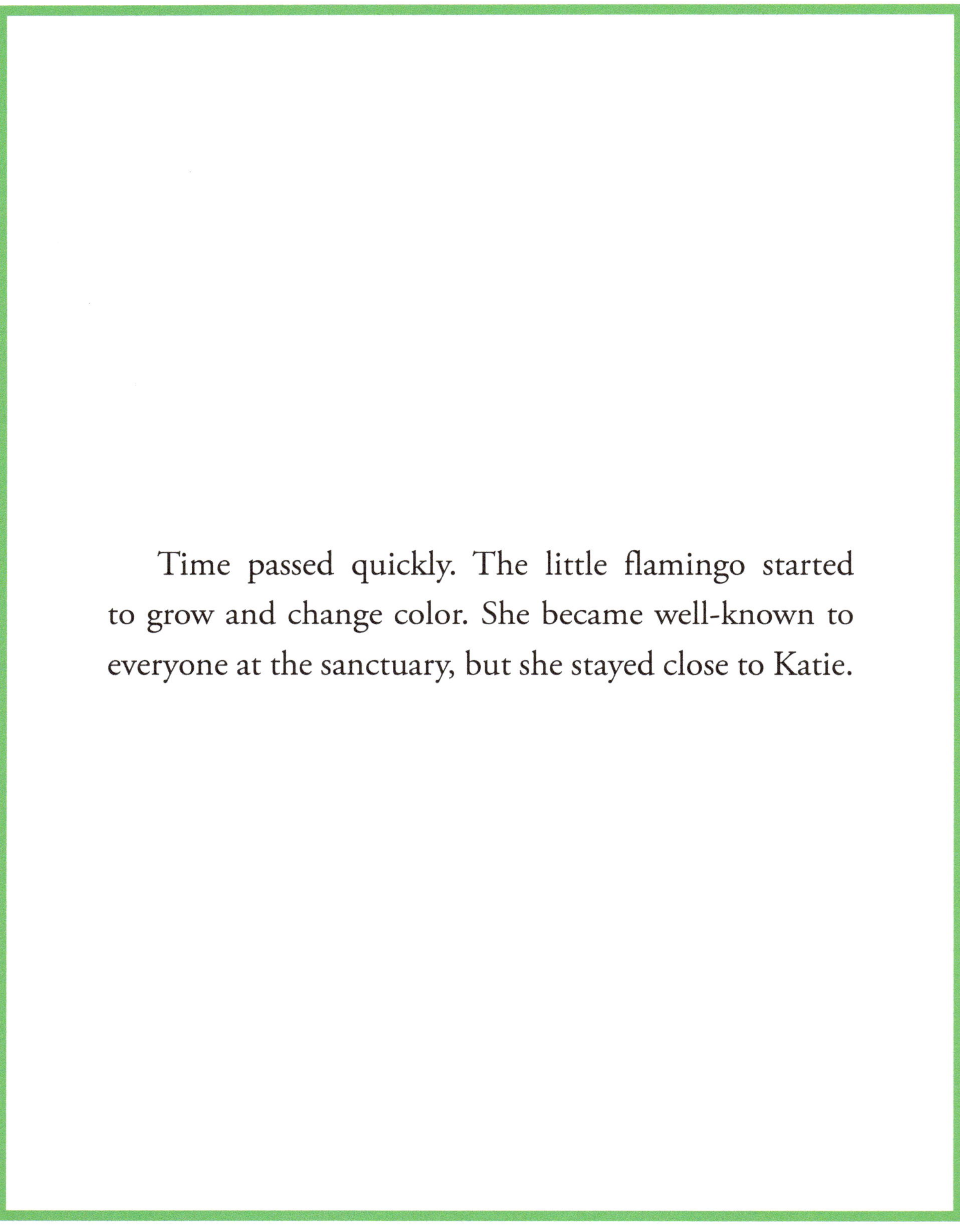

Time passed quickly. The little flamingo started to grow and change color. She became well-known to everyone at the sanctuary, but she stayed close to Katie.

She was a nosy little bird. One day, while Katie was working, she disappeared. Katie knew that if a box was open, she had her nose in it, just to see what was inside. Sure enough, at the back of her office was a big open box. Guess who was in there?

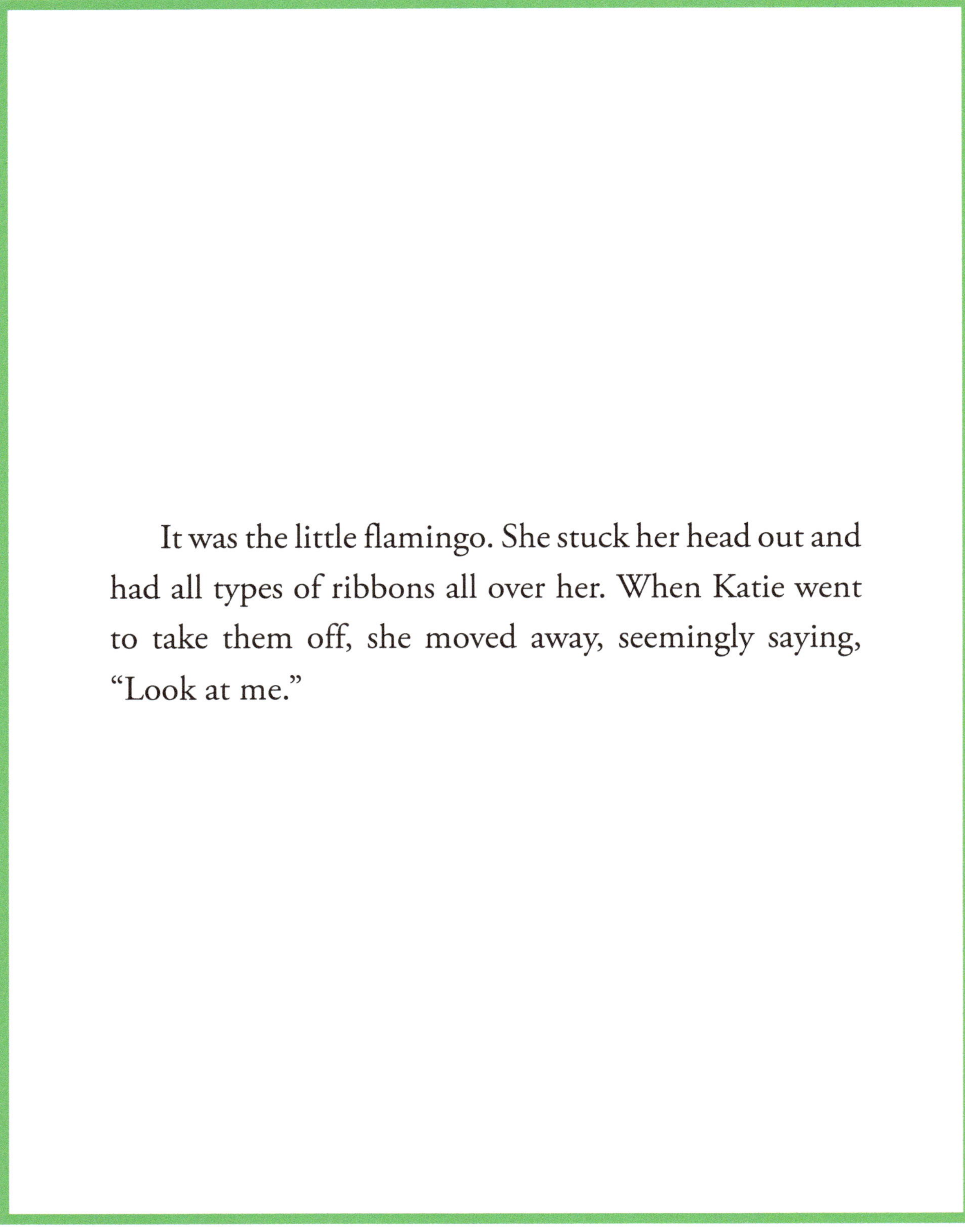

It was the little flamingo. She stuck her head out and had all types of ribbons all over her. When Katie went to take them off, she moved away, seemingly saying, "Look at me."

Every day, there was something new with Lainey: ribbons, flowers, anything for attention. Katie happened to notice Lainey when the radio was on playing music. Lainey had this little strut she would do. So Katie got her a red tutu and ballerina slippers. Wow! Lainey was in heaven.

Katie said, "I see you like to be noticed. You are quite a character." Anytime she found any type of fabric or loose ribbon, she had it. Katie said, "We have to find a name for you, little one." Katie thought and remembered when she and a friend played dress-up. Her friend Lainey loved the attention she got from dressing up, so she named the little flamingo Lainey.

Nothing was the same at the bird sanctuary. Lainey was a hit with everyone. She was growing into a very pretty pink flamingo. One morning, Katie couldn't find her sun hat and sunglasses. Lainey had them. So Katie fastened the glasses and hat on Lainey, and that was it. Lainey was hooked on that attire; she was so cool. When Lainey is in the pool with the other flamingos, you can always tell who Lainey is: she will have her cool shades and sun hat on.

About the Author

Karen is a retired clinical pharmacy technician. She does her writing as a hobby of sorts. She and her dog Bella live in a small coal-mining town, and they enjoy the outdoors when she is not writing.